FIGS *in* BLOOM

Fostering Independence Growth
and Spirituality in Teenage Girls

BOBI GENTRY GOODWIN

FIGS in Bloom
Fostering Independence, Growth, and Spirituality in God's Precious Girls.

Copyright © 2023 by Bobi Gentry Goodwin

Paperback ISBN: 979-8-9879908-1-0

Ebook ISBN: 979-8-9879908-0-3

Published by BGG Publications
San Francisco Bay Area, California

Visit Bobi Gentry Goodwin online to learn more at bobigentrygoodwin.com

Printed in the United States of America

Table of Contents

FIGS Bible Study Lessons

To all who have struggled to find the Way.

Introduction

No good tree bears bad fruit, nor does a bad tree bear good fruit. Each tree is recognized by its own fruit. People do not pick figs from thornbushes, or grapes from briers. A good man brings good things out of the good stored up in his heart, and an evil man brings evil things out of the evil stored up in his heart. For the mouth speaks what the heart is full of. – Luke 6:43-45

The *FIGS in Bloom Small Group Curriculum* was birthed out of the desire to start a small in-home Bible study group for my daughter and her friends. The curriculum is designed to incorporate fun, food, laughter, and biblical instruction to create a memorable experience that helps both participants and leaders better understand their place in God's heart through the Bible's most beloved personalities.

Each lesson is focused on content awareness and fun activities that reinforce thematic and biblical instruction. The curriculum is set over one year with a lesson plan for each month. The lessons can also be used to conduct a twelve-week study.

My daughter, her friends, and my co-facilitators all had a blast engaging in these lessons within our small group of middle school girls, so I wanted to share the information with Bible-believing leaders who desire to **F**oster **I**ndependence, **G**rowth, and **S**pirituality in God's precious girls.

All lessons include:

- Group Structure

- Quarterly Theme

- Lesson Topic

- Bible Personality

- Quarterly Memory Scripture

- Group Game Activity

- Journal Entry Activity

- Musical Playlist

The FIGS Bible study leader's guide is arranged in three main sections. First, we'll outline the FIGS Bible study environment and overall group meeting agenda to help you create a comfortable, structured, fun learning environment for the girls.

Then, we'll discuss the structure and key elements of the curriculum used to engage participants with the content of each lesson. Last, we'll go through the details of each lesson.

I pray the FIGS Bible study will help both leaders and young girls learn more about themselves, each other, and who they are as daughters of the Most High King

Scan this code with your mobile device for the FIGS welcome video for group leaders.

Letter to Group Leaders and Participants

Dear Child of God:

Growing up has its perks and disadvantages. My teenage years were full of highs and lows. Middle school was a time of first experiences. In the sixth grade, I learned to iron clothes, make bubbles with my chewing gum, and pop a wheely on my bike. The seventh grade was full of adventures, including wearing my hair down, applying make-up, and growing my fingernails as long as I could. By the time I reached eighth grade I held hands with several boyfriends, watched a ton of scary movies, and had more than a few zits.

The early teenage years of my life were also peppered with challenging times. On most days, I would find myself alone with no one to talk to. I had heard about Jesus Christ, but He was just some big guy in the sky. My grandmother had taken me to church, and I just didn't get it. Sitting in some grand building while my grandmother and her friends sang songs, waved their hands, and told me to sit still was simply no fun. I couldn't wait to get out of there and get back home. I spent most of my time at home, anyway.

Home was where I was most comfortable. By the time I was twelve, I had undergone two surgeries. Most of my older siblings had left home, and my parents were arguing a lot. I was used to sitting at home alone, but I wasn't used to being lonely. When my parents argued, I did not have anyone else I felt I could trust except that big guy in the sky.

To my surprise, we had great conversations. I would tell Him how I felt and end up feeling a lot less lonely and afraid. My conversations with Jesus Christ helped me through some of the best and worst times of my life. Sure, at the time I did not know about the Apostle Paul, Abigail, or the prophet Jeremiah. I only knew that Jesus was always there for me, and that was all I needed to know.

As I grew older, I leaned on Him even more. I found comfort in Jesus when I had to take a hard test, got bullied in high school, started my first job, and moved away for college. The conversations that started years ago multiplied as my days went on. Attending church to learn more about Jesus energized my faith in Him, but it was not until I started reading the Bible that I learned just what an impact Jesus could have on my daily life.

I learned the people in the Bible were just like me. Discovering that Abraham had to move away from his family encouraged me. I learned from Jacob and Esau that fighting with my brothers is not unusual. I was also amazed that Gideon struggled with confidence, as I did.

The Bible also taught me a lot about who I was meant to be. Knowing that the Lord can give me power like Elijah, wisdom like Solomon, forgiveness like David, or influence like Paul energized me. I learned so much from reading the Bible and the people tucked within its pages that I wanted to share just a little bit of it with you, too. Because out of all that I discovered, I am most grateful that Jesus Christ is the same as when I met Him as a tween for the very first time: Jesus Christ is love.

He loves me and He loves you too.

In Him,

Bobi

FIGS

BIBLE STUDY
LEADER'S GUIDE

The FIGS Meeting Environment

Teacher Tactics

The FIGS meeting environment is designed to help leaders create clear expectations and a fun learning routine for all participants.

Please open each group meeting with prayer. Group participants should be encouraged to sit in a circle to provide a supportive container where everyone can see one another. As a group leader, you will begin the discussions and then transition to facilitator and guide as you encourage the girls to participate. FIGS is designed for participants and leaders to learn from each other, so questions, open dialogue, curiosity, and laughter are always encouraged.

Clear expectations and mutual respect are pillars of the FIGS group process. It is essential to formulate rules with input and agreement by all participants. Either post the rules or provide a copy to each participant to review as a group following the opening prayer.

Cellular phones should be discouraged. It's recommended to collect cell phones from participants before group meetings begin. It may help to offer rewards or points incentives in exchange for the phones. All group members' parents or caregivers should be alerted to the cell phone policy. Group leaders are also encouraged to provide their contact info to all parents or caregivers, but refrain from cell phone usage themselves.

All group members should be encouraged to speak throughout every session. During the first few sessions, guides may choose to reward participation with incentives such as candy, reward points, thank you's, or applause. Begin with a check-in by giving each guide and participant a few moments to share about their week. Check-in is a time to listen, reflect, so problem-solving is discouraged. Thank each participant for sharing to help foster warmth, encouragement, and ongoing dialogue.

Repetition is an integral part of the FIGS group study. Memory scriptures should be discussed and reviewed at each meeting. Group participants should be rewarded for memorization. Group leaders can also display the memory scripture during each meeting for the group to recite.

Topic and thematic reviews are also key teaching tools for participants. Leaders can promote thematic understanding and application with well-scripted life examples. The arrangement of the topics and themes is designed as a progression to encourage understanding and acceptance for all participants. Academic and friendship environments can be difficult to manage for students, so FIGS group leaders must provide both educational information and a safe space for participants to learn and ask questions. Jesus is relational, so the goal of FIGS is to build relationships.

Students spend most of their time in social environments around dynamic personalities. Therefore, FIGS should be a fun experience where the Bible personalities come alive. Group leaders are encouraged to participate in Scripture reading, discussion, and Bible personality highlights. It's important to facilitate non-judgmental dialogue that explores how the character may have felt, what they may have done, and how their environment may have impacted their choices.

FIGS Meeting Agenda

All group meetings should keep the same structure, so participants know what to expect. Familiarity and group norms facilitate a sense of safety among group participants. Group surprises are discouraged except on review nights.

Group Introductions

All group members (including leaders) will introduce herself, including what school she attends, her grade level, and one favorite (color, food, song, etc.) for the week.

Group Rules

During the first meeting, leaders will encourage each member to contribute one rule for the group. Make sure a scribe documents the rules for review during future meetings.

Group Check-In

All members, (including leaders) will participate in a group check-in regarding her feelings and how her week has gone. Each member can rate her week using a 1-10 scale, while leaders encourage each girl to elaborate on her rating. Candy or fruit snacks can be provided as incentives. A feelings list is provided later in this curriculum.

Review Memory Scripture

A memory scripture is provided for each quarter in the "Memorizing God's Word" section of this curriculum. Group members should review the memory scripture at each meeting.

Review Topic

Leaders will review the designated topic of the evening with the group.

Theme

Group leaders will plan and implement activities, discussion, and life application examples around the quarterly theme.

Biblical Study

The heart of each lesson is the corresponding Biblical personality study. Read and review the key scripture. Themes and questions have been provided as examples of dialogue and study.

Game Activity

Each lesson includes one suggested group game activity. Other game ideas are provided in the Game Time section of this curriculum for variety or group leader variation.

Snack

Each group meeting should include a light snack or dinner for group participants.

Prayer

Each group meeting begins and ends in prayer. Group members should be encouraged to join hands in a circle and pray together as led by group leaders or volunteer group members.

Curriculum Review Nights

On curriculum review nights, group members or leaders will choose a topic that highlights a quarterly theme.

Journal Entry

Each lesson includes one suggested journal assignment for the girls to complete as homework.

Playlist

Each lesson includes a playlist. Group participants are encouraged to listen to the playlist prior to the next group meeting. Group leaders can also use playlists in the group meeting setting, during game activities, or to generate points for group members.

The FIGS Bible Study Structure

Teacher Tactics

Now that we've discussed the environment, we'll get into the agenda and key elements of the FIGS Bible Study. Teaching young people about the Bible has been one of my greatest pleasures. I have enjoyed every moment and my prayer is that you will too. Please approach each lesson with joy, curiosity, and an open heart and mind. Jesus led with love, and we can too.

It is time to have some fun! The Bible is not boring. On the contrary, it is an exciting book to read and even more fascinating to study. The Bible is filled with stories of love, conflict, hope, hardship, courage, compassion, and miracles. It is a compilation of books inspired by God in which historical accounts of people, places, and personalities jump right off the page.

Group leaders are encouraged to make the Bible lessons come alive for participants by illuminating different Bible personalities and their life experiences. The people highlighted in the Word of God are just like us in many ways. They live in communities, are surrounded by culture, have jobs, love their families, and struggle with the issues of life. In His Word, God shows us that not only does He understand our joys and pains, but He loves us through them. He is and will always be for us.

In the next section, you will learn the steps for each Bible study.

FIGS Bible Study Agenda

Personality Introduction

Begin by introducing the Bible personality. Each lesson includes background information, ministry highlights, Bible contemporaries, and other helpful information to inspire discussion.

Scripture Reading

All group members should be supplied with Bibles if possible. Each group member should read a portion of the scripture pertaining to the lesson.

Group Review

Facilitate discussion and understanding by encouraging group members to summarize the scripture reading.

Group Discussion

Encourage and facilitate members in a lively discussion about the lesson material, including life application examples, topic ideas, and Bible personality key points. The discussion is also the time to bridge scripture with other content in the lesson, including the topic, theme, journal prompt, and other fun activities.

Group Game

Discuss the group game activity to contextualize the lesson.

Take Home Journal Entry

Photocopy the journal prompt pages and provide each participant with a copy to take home for additional growth and exploration.

Lesson Plans

Month	Lesson	Theme	Topic	Bible Personality
January	1	Awareness	Vision	Timothy
February	2		Vices	Mary/Martha
March	3		Review	Review
April	4	Behavior	Courage	Esther
May	5		Confidence	David
June	6		Review	Review
July	7	Character	Grace	Naomi
August	8		Gifts	Joseph
September	9		Review	Review
October	10	Discipleship	Prayer	Hannah
November	11		Praise/ Worship	Daniel
December	12		Review	Review

Quarterly Lesson Review

Teacher Tactics

The rhythm of the FIGS Bible study consists of two character studies, followed by a week of review. Review nights are open slots in the curriculum intended for leaders and participants to revisit the preceding lessons, underscore takeaways, and discuss life applications in their one unique way. Here are a few suggestions for how to make memories during review nights.

Lesson reviews can be a fun time for group leaders to cultivate their creativity in thematic instruction by expressing their desires and ideas for games, playlists, or instruction as they are comfortable.

Review nights can also be used for additional group times to foster incentivized games for group participants.

Plan a fun, creative party for the girls. They may be allowed to invite a friend or sibling for crafts or a holiday-theme.

Give the girls the opportunity for their creativity and flexibility to shine by allowing them to lead the group using a similar group structure. Social media applications can also be encouraged on review nights to play games or highlight lessons.

Each of the next four sections unveils a key element of the FIGS Bible study used to help instructors create engaging, memorable experiences for the girls: Scripture memorization, labeling emotions, game time, and praise and worship.

Memorizing God's Word

Teacher Tactics

Scripture memorization is an essential part of the FIGS curriculum, both during the group process, and for each of the girls to hold God's Word in her heart long after group meetings have concluded.

Reinforcing the importance of God's Word among group members in a fun way can promote comfort and familiarity with the Bible, and reinforce the power of Scripture.

There are many ways to encourage and help the girls memorize Scripture.

- Display Scripture during meetings.

- Pop-quiz the girls and provide an incentive or reward to encourage group participants to memorize Scriptures.

- Prepare flash cards for at-home study.

- Provide incentives for reciting Scripture, such as a treat, a prize, or points to be tallied and redeemed for prizes at the end of quarter.

- Send memory scriptures in birthday cards or notes to the girls, even after the group concludes.

Memory Scriptures

Theme	Scripture
Awareness	For I know the plans I have for you, declares the LORD, plans to prosper you and not to harm you, plans to give you hope and a future (Jeremiah 29:11).
Behavior	But God demonstrates his own love for us in this: While we were still sinners, Christ died for us (Romans 5:8).
Character	I praise you because I am fearfully and wonderfully made; your works are wonderful, I know that full well (Psalms 139:14).
Discipleship	A new command I give you: Love one another. As I have loved you, so you must love one another (John 13:34).

Labeling Emotions

Teacher Tactics

Young people are at varying stages of identifying and using language to label and express emotions. Complex feelings can easily overwhelm a girl's ability to navigate social situations, so the FIGS curriculum provides a space for group members to communicate their emotions in a safe, social environment.

Emotional intelligence takes practice and intentionality. Group leaders are encouraged to help participants gain social and communication skills by expressing their feelings in a non-judgmental environment that fosters the love of God while underscoring His ability to handle, accept, and illuminate all types of emotions in His Word.

Feelings List

Angry	Determined	Hurt	Regretful
Arrogant	Disappointed	Jealous	Relieved
Bashful	Disbelieving	Joyful	Sad
Beautiful	Disgusted	Lonely	Satisfied
Blissful	Embarrassed	Loved	Scared
Bored	Excited	Mad	Shocked
Brave	Exhausted	Mindful	Strong
Bullied	Frustrated	Miserable	Surprised
Calm	Goofy	Optimistic	Sympathetic
Cautious	Grieving	Passionate	Tranquil
Concerned	Guilty	Peaceful	Victimized
Confident	Happy	Pessimistic	Victorious
Confused	Hopeful	Positive	Wonderful
Curious	Humorous	Powerful	Worried

Time to Grow

Teacher Tactics

Studying the Word of God produces change in every believer. Students of the Bible learn about God's goodness and His righteousness. The FIGS curriculum encourages group leaders to highlight biblical and topical instruction through the lens of overarching themes that promote right living.

Four themes were chosen to help leaders foster growth among the girls. Group participants should leave the twelve-week study with improved skills in Awareness, Behavior, Character, and Discipleship (A, B, C, Ds). The earlier students are taught the A, B, C, Ds, the quicker they will learn and master them.

Each skill is backed by Scripture.

A= Awareness

"The wisdom of the prudent is to give thought to their ways, but the folly of fools is deception" (Proverbs 14:8).

B= Behavior

"Don't let anyone look down on you because you are young, but set an example for the believers in speech, in conduct, in love, in faith and in purity" (1 Timothy 4:12).

C= Character

"Not only so, but we also glory in our sufferings, because we know that suffering produces perseverance; perseverance, character; and character, hope. And hope does not put us to shame, because God's love has been poured out into our hearts through the Holy Spirit, who has been given to us" (Romans 5:3-5).

D= Discipleship

"By this everyone will know that you are my disciples, if you love one another"(John 13:35).

Game Time

Teacher Tactics

Group games should be a time of excitement. Instead of teaching, FIG group leaders can take a back seat and watch the fun unfold. Some games require leader participation. For other games, leaders will check in with participants or simply join in the fun and banter.

Leaders will take an opportunity to link the group game to the lesson as the games wrap up. Typically, games are followed by dinner or a snack.

Group Game Activities

Vision Board

Each group member creates a vision board using content cut outs from magazines, newspapers, or other pictures. A vision board is a poster board designed with the students' wants, desires, or needs for the future.

Jellybeans

Group leaders provide any type of mixed jellybeans. Assorted flavored jellybeans work best. Group leaders mix up jellybeans and allow girls to grab the same number of jellybeans that are in the group. The girls eat and describe what the jellybean looked like and if the taste matched their vision for bean. This activity can also be done with baby food where the girls blind-taste and guess the food.

Famous Personalities

Tape a cutout of a celebrity on each girl's back. Popular personalities to schoolgirls at the current time work great, but group leaders can also mix in Bible personalities as well. Each girl must ask questions until the girl wearing the personality figures out which celebrity photo is taped to her back.

Make-Up Stations

Group members are encouraged to bring their make-up to the group meeting. Separate the girls into teams of two or three. Each team applies make-up to one team member, but she is not allowed to see her face until all make-up is applied, at which time she judges if this is how she likes to see herself. Guide the girls into a discussion to reflect and explain if other people's vision of her really reflects who she is.

Charades

Traditional Game

Jenga by Hasbro

Traditional Game

Wake Up

Separate the girls into two teams. Each group participant from the opposite team takes a turn laying down. The other group team members surround her and take turns trying to make the girl laugh. The team that wakes up the most participants wins.

Write a Letter to Your Future Self

Instruct the girls to write a one-page letter to their future self, ideally at age thirty. Then the girls work together to write Jesus's letter to His 30-year-old self from the viewpoint of their current age.

S'mores

Each group participant can assemble smores contents in a sandwich bag for each of their teachers. The girls may also decorate the bags and include a thank you note.

Wink Game

Leaders choose a member of the group to be "Judas." All the girls assemble in a circle. "Judas" winks unsuspectedly at their group members in the circle and "kills" them with a wink. Person who was "killed" must leave the group while the other group members guess who the "Judas" is.

Stomp the Yard

Group members should be separated into teams, blow up balloons and place numbers in them according to colors. Each team picks a color and then outside, the girls try to smash opposing teams' balloons. Each team with the most points from the opposite teams' numbers wins.

Glasses Game

Each girl is provided with eyeglasses, a pen and sticky notes. She writes something negative she has heard or believes about herself on a sticky note and sticks it to the eyeglasses. She then walks to the other side of the room wearing the glasses. She removes the sticky note and disposes of it before returning to the other side of the room.

Match Game

Each girl writes a positive statement about herself and other group members on sticky notes. The girls place the sticky notes all over the room, return to their seats, and then close their eyes for twenty seconds. When they open their eyes, they may be unleashed to find sticky notes that match in pairs of two. The girl with the most matching sticky notes wins.

Leader Game

The Leader Game is good old-fashioned Simon Says with a twist: all the girls are blind-folded except the girl leading the game.

Follow the Leader

Place a variety of ingredients used to bake things on a table. Divide the girls into teams of two. Each team will choose a team leader. The leader is then given a box of cake mix, but is allowed is allowed to look at cake mix box for thirty-three seconds after which she must instruct her team how to make the cake. This game can also be done with other assembly items like puzzles, with only the team leader allowed to look at the puzzle.

Positive Affirmations/Mason Jar

Each group participant writes positive affirmations on slips of paper and fills a mason jar to the top for a special teacher, principal, or pastor. Jars can also be decorated.

Praise and Worship

Teacher Tactics

Young people enjoy listening to music. Many pop in their head-phones and zone out. The FIGS curriculum developer built a curated playlist of worship music to help the girls both zone out and tune in to each Bible lesson.

Group leaders can play praise and worship music during their study or game times. Leaders are also encouraged to rec-ommend group participants listen to songs from the selected playlist to help encourage them encounter God in a different way. The girls may also listen to playlists while completing journal writing assignments.

Suggested Playlists

Lesson 1 Topic: Vision
Track 1: Good Good Father by Chris Tomlin
Track 2: What You're Worth by Mandisa
Track 3: Do Life Big by Jaime Grace

Lesson 2 Topic: Vices
Track 1: Good Fight by Unspoken
Track 2: Victory by Tye Tribett
Track 3: I Surrender by V. Rose

Lesson 3 Topic: Review
Track 1: Nothing Ever by Citizen Way
Track 2: God is on the Move by 7eventh Time Down
Track 3: Build my Life by Bri Babineaux

Lesson 4 Topic: Courage
Track 1: The River by Jordan Feliz
Track 2: Can't Give Up Now by Mary Mary
Track 3: I Believe it Now by Sideway Prophets & Olivia Lane

Lesson 5 Topic: Confidence
Track 1: Hello Fear by Kirk Franklin
Track 2: Nobody by Casting Crowns
Track 3: Gold by Britt Nicole

Lesson 6 Topic: Review
Track 1: Even if by MercyMe
Track 2: Overcoming by William McDowell & Martha Munizzi
Track 3: Imperfect Me by Smokie Norful

Lesson 7 Topic: Grace
Track 1: Until Grace by Tauren Grace
Track 2: Grace by Jonathan McReynolds
Track 3: Broken People (feat. DOE) by Israel & New Breed

Lesson 8 Topic: Gifts
Track 1: Intentional by Travis Greene
Track 2: E6 by Evvie McKinney
Track 3: Blessings by Lecrae

Lesson 9 Topic: Review
Track 1: You Say by Lauren Daigle
Track 2: Never Lost by Tribl & Marverick City Music
Track 3: Goodness of God by CeCe Winans

Lesson 10 Topic: Prayer
Track 1: Haven't Seen it yet by Danny Gokey
Track 2: Pray by Koryn Hawthorne
Track 3: Find You on my Knees by Kari Jobe

Lesson 11 Topic: Praise
Track 1: Put a Praise on it by Tasha Cobbs Leonard (Feat. Kierra Sheard)
Track 2: I'm Yours by Casey J
Track 3: Jireh by Maverick City Music (Feat. Chandler Moore & Naomi Raine)

Lesson 12 Topic: Review
Track 1: Fix my Eyes by King & Country

Track 2: Your Great Name by Natalie Grant
Track 3: Take Me to the King by Tamela Mann

FIGS

BIBLE STUDY
LESSONS

Lesson 1

Timothy

Bible Personality
Timothy

Scripture
Each group member should read a portion of scripture pertaining to tonight's lesson.

Topic
Vision: The act or power of seeing: Sight. [1]

Theme
Awareness

Scripture Reading
2 Timothy 1:1-14

Scripture Summary

Paul is an apostle and teacher of the Word of God, but he cannot do it alone. Throughout his journey, he encountered incredible people who helped him along the way. One of those people was Timothy.

Timothy was a young man raised to believe in Jesus Christ by his mother and grandmother. He also learned the Holy Scriptures. Paul and Timothy were more than friends or even mentor and mentee. Their bond resembled a father-son relationship, so it hurt to be separated.

Paul remembered and prayed for Timothy. As his mentor and father in the faith, Paul hoped Timothy would have a wonderful relationship with God. He wants his son Timothy to know what a treasure he is and what kind of special gifts God stored inside him. Paul didn't want him to be afraid. He wanted Timothy to be fearless in knowing that God loves him and gave him power, self-discipline, and the capacity to love.

Paul encouraged Timothy that no matter what, he should not be ashamed of himself, Paul, or God. Instead, he should live his life in holiness through God's grace for him and all people. Paul reminded Timothy to never forget what he learned and to guard it with the help of the Holy Spirit.

Key Points

Timothy was a young man who devoted his life to Christ. He was raised in a home with parents from two different cultures. His maternal relatives instructed Timothy in the Scriptures from an early age. Timothy eventually left home to travel with his mentor Paul to share the Gospel.

Possible Talking Points

- Timothy's youth

- Planning for the future

- Timothy's genuine faith

- Living in communities where cultures clash

- Taking risks

- Creating valuable relationships

- Sharing the Good News

Leader Notes

_____

_____

_____

_____

_____

_____

_____

_____

_____

_____

_____

_____

Discussion

1. Who was Timothy's friend?

2. Why was this letter written to Timothy?

3. What was Timothy's friend's vision for him?

4. What are your friends' and family's visions for you? How would they describe you?

5. What traits do you want others to know about you?

Game Suggestion

Vision Board

Journal Question

Timothy left his grandmother, Lois, and mother, Eunice, to pursue the ministry of Jesus Christ. What do you have to leave behind to follow your vision?

_____

_____

_____

_____

_____

_____

_____

_____

_____

_____

Lesson 2

Mary & Martha

Bible Personalities
Mary and Martha

Scripture
Each group member reads a portion of scripture pertaining to tonight's lesson.

Topic
Vices: A habitual and usually trivial defect or shortcoming: Foible.[1]

Theme
Awareness

Scripture Reading
Luke 10:38-42

Scripture Summary

Mary and Martha were sisters. They lived together with their brother Lazarus. Like many sisters, they experienced sibling rivalry, especially when they didn't see eye to eye.

Martha, the oldest sister, found herself busy cleaning the house for their guests while her younger sister sat around. Martha did not appreciate having to do all the work. She wanted her sister to help, and she knew exactly what to do to get her attention. She would tell their Lord Jesus. Surely, Jesus would tell her sister to help.

Jesus answered Martha, but not like she thought. He informed her not to be so worried. He reminded Martha that instead of worrying about so many things, she should take to take time with the things that matter. Jesus declared Mary was indeed doing the right thing. Although she was not helping Martha, she instead chose to spend quality time in a relationship with Him.

Key Points

Mary and Martha were sisters, but they had totally different personalities. Mary was relational and Martha was purposeful and all about action. Both sisters had different goals and ways of interacting with people. They lived together and hosted celebrations for those in their communities, but sometimes their personalities clashed.

Possible Talking Points

- Inaccurate perceptions

- Personality Types

- Sibling relationships

- Conflict resolution

- Feeling undervalued

- Self-care

- Hospitality

Leader Notes

_____

_____

_____

_____

_____

_____

_____

_____

_____

_____

_____

_____

Discussion

1. Who are you more like, Mary or Martha? How is each lady unique?

2. Which lady would you like to have as a friend? What are their vices?

3. How do you handle conflict?

4. How did Jesus show He cared about both ladies?

5. What do you do when you are worried, angry, misunderstood, or feel frustrated?

Game Suggestion

Make-Up Stations

Journal Question

Martha was angry with her sister, Mary, and Jesus reminded her to enjoy life and worry less. What do you need to worry about less to enjoy life more?

_____

_____

_____

_____

_____

_____

_____

_____

_____

_____

Lesson 3

Review

Bible Personality
Review

Scripture
Review

Theme
Awareness

Discussion
Open

Potential Key Points
Open

Game Suggestion
Open

Journal Question

Write memory Scripture in your own words. What does this Scripture mean to you?

"For I know the plans I have for you," declares the Lord, "plans to prosper you and not to harm you, plans to give you hope and a future." Jeremiah 29:11

_____

_____

_____

_____

_____

_____

_____

_____

_____

_____

_____

Lesson 4

Esther

Bible Personality
Esther

Scripture
Each group member reads a portion of scripture pertaining to tonight's lesson.

Topic
Courage: Mental or moral strength to venture, persevere, and withstand danger, fear, or difficulty. [1]

Theme
Behavior

Scripture Reading
Esther 4:3-17

Scripture Summary

An entire community was in mourning. Queen Esther was informed by her staff that her cousin Mordecai was also in great distress. Esther wanted to do something to help him. As the wife of the king, she was the only person in her family with access to power. Esther sent clothes to her cousin Mordecai after she heard how upset he was, but he refused.

Queen Esther could not figure out what upset her cousin so she sent her staff to find out. She learned the king had sent out an order for all Jewish people to be killed. Esther and her family were Jewish, but the king did not know. Hardly anyone knew that the young queen of Persia was Jewish.

Mordecai sent her clear instructions on how she could use her power to intervene, but Esther was scared. It had been a long time since she had seen her husband and she wouldn't dare barge in on him, after all, he was the king. But Mordecai would not take no for an answer. He cautioned her to summon her courage because she may have been put in power for this very reason. Esther knew what she had to do. She had to use her power to stand up for her people, no matter what the cost.

Key Points

Esther was an unlikely queen. Her parents died when she was very young, so her cousin Mordecai raised her and gave her a comfortable home. Esther was chosen out of scores of young women to be taken to the palace, where she found favor with the royal staff and with the king himself. She was quickly thrust into a world of opulence, royalty, and tradition. Her new life was filled with blessings, but all the while she was burdened with a secret. She was not allowed to tell anyone she was Jewish.

Possible Talking Points

- Courage

- Fear

- Power and Control

- Injustice

- Self- Esteem

- Taking action to help others

- God's plan for our lives

Leader Notes

Discussion

1. What do you think happened to Esther after her people were saved?

2. How do you handle fear?

3. What are some difficult things about listening to authority figures?

4. Describe the most courageous act you have ever seen or heard of.

5. What is salvation? How did Jesus show courage on the cross?

Game Suggestion

Glasses Game

Journal Question

Esther had to face her fears to help her people. What fears do you need to face today to help yourself or others?

_____

_____

_____

_____

_____

_____

_____

_____

_____

_____

_____

Lesson 5

David

Bible Personality
David

Scripture
Each group member reads a portion of scripture pertaining to
tonight's lesson.

Topic
Confidence: A feeling or consciousness of one's powers or of
reliance on one's circumstances.[1]

Theme
Behavior

Scripture Reading
1 Samuel 17:12-37

Scripture Summary

David was the youngest child of eight sons. His three other brothers had already joined King Saul's army to defend the nation from the Philistines. David lived at home and helped his elderly father, Jesse, with their livestock.

He frequently traveled to the battlefield to bring supplies to his brothers and the Israelite army, and to bring back a report to Jesse about his sons. Traveling back and forth from home to the battlefield couldn't be easy, but David listened to his father.

One day, during a delivery to the battlefield, David heard a commotion. A Philistine giant named Goliath was bullying the Israelite army, and they were scared. The army retreated even though the King Saul offered a handsome reward to anyone who would defeat the giant.

David could not believe these happenings. This giant was one man against the God of Israel and there was even a reward to defeat him. He had heard all that he needed to hear. He told other soldiers he would fight Goliath. David's brother over-heard him and became angry, but David did not let his brother deter him. He kept on talking and was soon summoned by King Saul. The young boy had courage in the Lord, so he agreed to fight the giant. David believed and was victorious.

Key Points

As the youngest son, he was discounted by many, but David was a young man with conviction. He was a hard worker, obedient to authority, and took his responsibilities seriously. He rose to the occasion despite many challenges. He believed in his God and himself instead of what other people thought of him.

Possible Talking Points

- Self Confidence

- Leadership

- Facing Obstacles

- Taking Responsibility

- Internal strength

- Being yourself

- Faith in God

Leader Notes

_____

_____

_____

_____

_____

_____

_____

_____

_____

_____

_____

Discussion

1. What are the giants in today's society?

2. Name a few young people that made great change.

3. What gives you confidence?

4. Give examples of experiences in David's life that could have made him lack confidence?

5. How does the perspective of others impact your peer group? How does the perspective of others impact you?

6. What is the difference between real versus perceived confidence?

Game Suggestion

Write a Letter to Your Future Self

Journal Question

David had confidence. Why do you think confidence is important to help people face difficult times? Where can you use more confidence in your own life?

_____

_____

_____

_____

_____

_____

_____

_____

_____

_____

_____

Lesson 6

Review

Bible Personality
Review

Scripture
Review

Theme
Behavior

Potential Key Points
Open

Discussion
Open

Game Suggestion
Open

Journal Question

Write memory Scripture in your own words. What does this Scripture mean to you?

But God demonstrates his own love for us in this: While we were still sinners, Christ died for us. Romans 5:8

Lesson 7

Naomi

Bible Personality
Naomi

Scripture
Each group member reads a portion of scripture pertaining to tonight's lesson.

Topic
Grace: A state of sanctification enjoyed through divine assistance.[1]

Theme
Character

Scripture Reading
Ruth 1:1-18

Scripture Summary

A severe famine ravaged the land. Like many families probably did, Elimelech, his wife, Naomi, and their two sons had to relocate to find food. They settled in the town of Moab. Unfortunately, tragedy struck when Elimelech died, leaving Naomi to care for her two sons. Soon her sons married Moabite women. They set out to enjoy life in their new land, but tragedy struck once again about ten years later when both of Naomi's sons died.

Naomi was a grieving woman. She had no one left other than her two daughters-in-law, Ruth and Orpah. She heard the Lord was blessing the people of her homeland with food, so she decided to return home. As a widow, it would have been very difficult for her to care for herself and her two daughters-in-law, so she sent the girls back to their families.

Naomi urged Ruth and Orpah to go back to their families so they could have a good life. When she kissed them goodbye, Ruth simply would not leave Naomi all by herself. Ruth insisted on following Naomi back to her homeland and wholeheartedly devoted herself to both Naomi and her God

Key Points

Naomi was a devoted mother who cared about her family. Life was good for Naomi until she experienced multiple tragedies. The death of her husband and her two sons impacted her life greatly. These traumas left her feeling bitter and despondent. In the midst of grief, she decided to move back to her home and encouraged her daughters-in-law to do the same.

Possible Talking Points

- Loyalty

- Faithfulness

- Coping skills

- Depression

- Helping others

- Family and Community

- Love

Leader Notes

_____

_____

_____

_____

_____

_____

_____

_____

_____

_____

_____

Discussion

1. How do you show love to others?

2. What characteristics make a good friend?

3. What does self-sacrifice mean?

4. How do you handle difficult situations?

5. What do you value in your relationship with others and with God?

Game Suggestion

Positive Affirmations/Mason Jar

Journal Question

Naomi lost almost everything in a short period of time. She had to find a way to rebuild her life in the face of loss. God showed her grace by giving her a new family. How does God show you grace through your relatives, friendships, or community?

_____

_____

_____

_____

_____

_____

_____

_____

_____

_____

_____

Lesson 8

Joseph

Bible Personality
Joseph

Scripture
Each group member reads a portion of scripture pertaining to tonight's lesson.

Topic
Gifts: A notable capacity, talent, or endowment.[1]

Theme
Character

Scripture Reading
Genesis 37

Scripture Summary

Joseph was his father's favorite of twelve sons. His father, Jacob, loved him so much that he had a special coat designed especially for him. This angered his other brothers, who were already jealous of him.

Joseph worked hard tending the sheep, but he also liked to talk. He told his father about the bad things his brothers did. He shared his dreams with his brothers, including dreams that demonstrated their resources bowing down to his. He even told his brothers about the dream where the sun, moon, and eleven stars bowed before him. No one likes to be considered second fiddle, so Joseph's brothers resented him all the more.

Family chores were common in Joseph's house. One day, when Joseph's brothers tended to the livestock, they saw Joseph leaving to go to the sheep pasture. The brothers were filled with such jealousy that most of them wanted to kill Joseph. Fortunately, not all brothers agreed. Reuben decided it would be best to just throw him in a cistern where he could rescue him later. Reuben saw traders approaching and decided they should sell him into slavery instead.

The brothers sold Joseph for twenty pieces of silver. Then, they dipped Joseph's special coat in goat's blood, and told their father he was dead. Their father believed the lie and was so overcome with grief that he tore his clothes and refused to be comforted. Joseph was eventually sold to the king's palace guard, where he lived for a long time.

Key Points

Joseph was a dreamer. God had gifted him with special abilities, and he was unashamed. He shared his dreams with
others even when they did not like what he had to say. He
struggled with relating to others, but he held fast to what he
believed was true.

Possible Talking Points

- Gifts and Abilities

- Standing for truth in the face of opposition

- Jealousy

- Communication skills

- Cruelty

- God's divine plan

- Forgiveness

Leader Notes

_____

_____

_____

_____

_____

_____

_____

_____

_____

_____

_____

Discussion

1. How can jealousy impact relationships?

2. Why is it important to help other people?

3. How has bullying impacted members of your school?

4. What does it mean to have a purpose?

5. Can you name your God-given talents or gifts that other people may envy?

Game Suggestion

Stomp the Yard

Journal Question

Joseph was a dreamer. God gave him special gifts and talents that he could use throughout his life. What gifts and talents do you think God has given you? Are you or others able to see them? Are there any gifts or talents you wish you had?

_____

_____

_____

_____

_____

_____

_____

_____

_____

_____

_____

_____

Lesson 9

Review

Bible Personality
Review

Scripture
Review

Theme
Character

Potential Key Points
Open

Discussion
Open

Game Suggestion
Open

Journal Question

Write memory Scripture in your own words. What does this Scripture mean to you?

I praise you because I am fearfully and wonderfully made; your works are wonderful, I know that full well. Psalms 139:14

_____

_____

_____

_____

_____

_____

_____

_____

_____

_____

_____

Lesson 10

Hannah

Bible Personality
Hannah

Scripture
Each group member reads a portion of scripture pertaining to tonight's lesson.

Topic
Prayer: The act or practice of praying to God or a god. [1]

Theme
Discipleship

Scripture Reading
1 Samuel 1:1-20

Scripture Summary

Multiple wives were common in the Old Testament times. Hannah was married to Elkanah, who had two sons with his other wife. Elkanah was a faithful man who took his wives and sons on a long journey to the tabernacle every year. As part of his worship to God, Elkanah always gave sacrifices to God for his family, but he gave more for Hannah because she had no children. Elkanah's other wife did not like this, so she got upset and bullied Hannah.

Hannah did not know what else to do, so after a meal, she headed to the entrance of the tabernacle to pray. She prayed fervently to the Lord through all of her tears. She asked the Lord for a son and vowed to dedicate him to the Lord for his entire life.

Eli the high priest saw her praying with so much passion that he scolded her for being drunk. Hannah corrected him and informed him of her passionate prayer. Eli was so touched by her tenacity that he prayed the Lord would grant her request and told her to go in peace. Hannah left the tabernacle encouraged. The Lord remembered Hannah's prayer, and when she got home from the tabernacle, she conceived a son she named Samuel.

Key Points

Hannah was a beautiful woman who wanted a child. She felt despondent because God did not give the one thing she wanted. She had a difficult time leaning into gratefulness because her desire was not fulfilled. She was also being taunted by those around her. She was loved by her husband but disliked by his other wife. She was stuck in a very hard place, and she knew her only way out was through the power of prayer.

Possible Talking Points

- Power of prayer

- Coping with disappointment

- God's Timing

- Dedication

- Depression

- Words of Encouragement

Leader Notes

Discussion

1. Why do people pray?

2. What did Hannah learn about prayer?

3. Is prayer important? Explain your answer.

4. Describe the importance of persevering despite obstacles.

5. Why do you think people do not pursue their goals and dreams?

Game Suggestion

Follow the Leader

Journal Question

Hannah had a life of prayer. She was not afraid to pray to God for what she wanted. How can prayer help or hinder you? Write three prayers that God can help you with.

_____

_____

_____

_____

_____

_____

_____

_____

_____

_____

_____

Lesson 11

Daniel

Bible Personality
Daniel

Scripture
Each group member reads a portion of scripture pertaining to tonight's lesson.

Topic
Praise: An expression of approval: Commendation. [1]

Worship: To honor or show reverence for as a divine being or supernatural power.[2]

Theme
Discipleship

Scripture Reading
Daniel 1:1-17

Scripture Summary

The beautiful Jerusalem was under siege by King Nebuchadnezzar of Babylon. He even captured some of the Israelite nobles to go through several years of training for service in his palace.

Daniel was identified as a young man suitable for training. They changed his name and gave him royal clothing. The king also provided him with wine and meat from the palace, but the Israelites had their own special diet as an act of worship to God. Daniel insisted on remaining loyal to God, so he refused the king's food.

Daniel asked the king's head servant to give him only vegetables and water, but the servant feared the king would get angry if Daniel and his friends looked weak. Daniel was a young man of conviction, so he negotiated a plan with the king's staff. Daniel and his friends would eat the meals allowed by their faith for ten days and then go through tests to judge how they looked compared to the men who ate the king's meals.

Daniel knew God would bless his faithfulness. At the end of the test, Daniel and his friends looked healthier and better nourished than the others. He passed the test and was allowed to keep his special diet. God also granted Daniel the ability to learn faster and even interpret visions and dreams.

Key Points

Daniel was exiled to another country. He found himself at odds with the customs and practices of his new homeland. He was raised and taught to follow God, but in his new home the people and culture were different. Daniel had to make some tough decisions really quickly. How could he continue to serve God and disobey the leaders in his new environment? He knew he couldn't. Daniel decided to remain faithful and worship God despite what anyone else said.

Possible Talking Points

- Difficult Choices

- Culture clashes

- Conviction

- Belief Systems

- Worship Practices

- God's provision and favor

- Faith

Leader Notes

Discussion

1. Would you rather play second string on a winning team or first string on a losing team?

2. What makes you unique?

3. What are the difficult aspects of being a leader?

4. Explain the benefits of determination.

5. What are you determined to do today? This month? This year? How can you make it happen?

6. How can you praise God with your actions?

Game Suggestion

Famous Personalities

Journal Question

Daniel worshipped and honored God with his mind and body. He decided to make worship a part of his daily life, even when others did not want him to. Why do you think Daniel thought worshipping God was so important? In what ways can you praise and worship God in your daily life?

_____

_____

_____

_____

_____

_____

_____

_____

_____

_____

_____

Lesson 12

Review

Bible Personality
Review

Scripture
Review

Theme
Discipleship

Potential Key Points
Open

Discussion
Open

Game Suggestion
Group Party

Journal Question

Write memory Scripture in your own words. What does this Scripture mean to you?

A new command I give you: Love one another. As I have loved you, so you must love one another. John 13:34

_____

_____

_____

_____

_____

_____

_____

_____

_____

_____

Farewell

As the rain and the snow come down from heaven, and do not return to it without watering the earth and making it bud and flourish so that it yields seed for the sower and bread for the eater, so is my word that goes out from my mouth: it will not return to me empty, but will accomplish what I desire and achieve the purpose for which I sent it. Isaiah 55:10-11

You did it! I am so proud of you and all the work you put in to organize, structure, teach, and disciple your FIGS in Bloom group. In all groups, there are clear wins and some losses. May you celebrate each win and hold them close to your heart.

I am certain you and the FIGS group accomplished so much. It is my sincerest hope that through this group your students have learned more about God, the Bible, and themselves. Always know that the intellect, growth, and spirituality you fostered by sharing the Word of God can never be erased.

God bless you and may His light shine through you always.

Warmly,

Bobi

FIGS

NOTES

Notes

Notes

Notes

Notes

Prayer to Start a Relationship with God

You can use this prayer as an example for your own prayer.

See Romans 10:9–10 for more about this relationship.

Dear God, I believe You are Lord. I acknowledge my sins before You now and ask I that You will forgive them. I turn away from my sins and turn my life into Your hands. I acknowledge You as Lord and confess that Jesus Christ is Your Son, who died on the cross, and You raised Him from the dead. Come into my heart. Lead and guide me always. I receive You by faith.

In Jesus's name.

Amen.

Acknowledgements

To my God,

Thank you. All the glory and honor belong to You. Great is thy faithfulness.

To my family,

Thank you for your love and patience.

To the FIGS and CIA Group Members,

Thank you for pushing me toward the more.

About the Author

Bobi Gentry Goodwin is a native of San Francisco. The Bay Area was where she first discovered her love for people and their stories. She has held a passion for writing since early child-hood. As a clinical social worker, her mission field is working with women and children. She is a wife and mother of two and an avid member of her local church. Bobi is a licensed minister, Bible study leader, and host of the Finding Forever Podcast. Her writing has been featured in *Chicken Soup for the Soul.* She is also a member of Delta Sigma Theta Sorority, Inc. Goodwin currently resides with her family in sunny California.

Also by Bobi Gentry Goodwin

Visit her at www.bobigentrygoodwin.com

Revelation by Bobi Gentry Goodwin

She Writes Press

$16.95, 978-1-63152-606-0

The lives of social worker Angela Lovelace and five-year-old boy Trevion are changed forever when they meet at the scene of his mother's death. While conducting her investigation, she discovers her father's picture at the site. Angela is a well-trained worker and never had a sleepless night until now as she grapples with this grim discovery. Fear, anxiety, and family secrets unfold as she sets out to uncover the truth.

Endnotes

1. Merriam-Webster.com Dictionary, s.v. "vision," accessed March 12, 2023, https://www.merriam-webster.com/dictionary/vision.

2. Merriam-Webster.com Dictionary, s.v. "vice," accessed March 12, 2023, https://www.merriam-webster.com/dictionary/vice.

3. Merriam-Webster.com Dictionary, s.v. "courage," accessed March 12, 2023, https://www.merriam-webster.com/dictionary/courage.

4. Merriam-Webster.com Dictionary, s.v. "confidence," accessed March 12, 2023, https://www.merriam-webster.com/dictionary/confidence.

5. Merriam-Webster.com Dictionary, s.v. "grace," accessed March 12, 2023, https://www.merriam-webster.com/dictionary/grace.

6. Merriam-Webster.com Dictionary, s.v. "gift," accessed March 12, 2023, https://www.merriam-webster.com/dictionary/gift.

7. Merriam-Webster.com Dictionary, s.v. "prayer," accessed March 12, 2023, https://www.merriam-webster.com/dictionary/prayer.

8. Merriam-Webster.com Dictionary, s.v. "praise," accessed March 12, 2023, https://www.merriam-webster.com/dictionary/praise.

9. Merriam-Webster.com Dictionary, s.v. "worship," accessed March 12, 2023, https://www.merriam-webster.com/dictionary/worship.